This book is due for return on or before the last date shown below

A Song for Owain

dinas

A Song for Owain

poems
in praise of
Owain Glyndŵr

edited by
Rhys Parry

Diolch i'r canlynol:

Gwasg Gomer am ganiatad i ddefnyddio cerddi Harri Webb, Iolo Goch,
Gwenallt a A. G. Prys-Jones

Seren am ganiatad i ddefnyddio 'Glyndŵr Subdued'
gan Steve Griffiths o'i *Selected Poems* (1993)

Glyndŵr Publishing am ganiatad i ddefnyddio 'Nationalism' gan Terry
Breverton o *The Path to Inexperience* (Wales Books, 2002)

J. M. Dent am ganiatad i ddefnyddio 'The Rising of Glyndŵr', 'Hyddgen',
a 'The Tree' gan R. S. Thomas o *Collected Poems, 1945-1990*
(Llundain, 1993)

Rhoddir yr elw o werthiant y llyfr hwn i Tŷ Hafan

Cover: Robat Gruffudd

ISBN: 0 86243 738 5

Dinas is an imprint of Y Lolfa

Printed and published in Wales
by Y Lolfa Cyf., Talybont, Ceredigion SY24 5AP
e-mail ylolfa@ylolfa.com
website www.ylolfa.com
tel. (01970) 832 304
fax 832 782

contents

Acknowledgements		8
Introduction		9
Llywelyn ap Gruffydd Fychan	*Nigel Jenkins*	13
Glyndŵr Road	*Mike Jenkins*	16
Rhyfela Hyd Farw	*Harri Webb*	18
By a Mountain Pool	*Harri Webb*	19
The Red, White and Green	*Harri Webb*	26
Owain Glyndŵr	*Harri Webb*	28
The Rising of Glyndŵr	*R. S. Thomas*	29
Hyddgen	*R. S. Thomas*	30
The Tree	*R. S Thomas*	31
A Ballad of Glyndŵr's Rising	*A. G. Prys-Jones*	34
Rebirth	*Terry Breverton*	36
Nationalism	*Terry Breverton*	38
In the Hill-country	*A. G. Prys-Jones*	40
The Passing of Owain Glyndŵr	*A. G. Prys-Jones*	42
Sycharth	*Byron Beynon*	44
Parliament House at Machynlleth	*Byron Beynon*	45
A Dried Deer Skin	*Ken Jones*	46
Sycharth	*Alan Wyke*	50

Achau Owain Glyndŵr	*Iolo Goch*	53
Moliant Owain Glyndŵr	*Iolo Goch*	57
Llys Owain Glyndŵr	*Iolo Goch*	60
Catrin Glyndŵr	*Menna Elfyn*	64
The Exile's Song	*Translated by Gillian Clarke*	65
Glyndŵr Subdued	*Steve Griffiths*	66
Bequeathed	*Robert King*	70
I Owain Glyndŵr	*Gruffudd Llwyd*	71
I Owain Glyndŵr	*Gruffudd Llwyd*	74
Remembrance	*John Parry*	78
Owain Glyndŵr	*Gwenallt*	80
Owain Glyndŵr	*Gwenallt*	82
On the Dedication of the Sword of State of Cymru	*Terry Breverton*	84
The Poems and the Poets		87

Annals of Owen Glyndŵr
(Peniarth MS. 135)

MCCCCXV yddaeth Owain mewn difant y gwyl vathe yn y
kynhayaf o hynny allan ni wybvwyd i ddifant rrann vawr a ddywaid i
varw y brudwyr a ddywedant na bv

*1415 Owen went into hiding on St. Matthew's Day in Harvest [Sept.21],
and thereafter his hiding place was unknown. Very many say that he died;
the seers [ie the poets] maintain he did not.*

'Glyndŵr is the undefeated symbol of Wales, with his red dragon of
Cadwaladr – he is the equivalent of Jeanne d'Arc and William
Wallace and el Cid for Welsh people everywhere.'
Gideon Brough, *Glyn Dŵr's War – the Campaigns of the last Prince of
Wales* (Wales Books, 2002)

In everlasting memory of the greatest freedom fighter of all time.

Dedicated to every man, woman and child who fell in the cause.

acknowledgements

My sincere thanks to the Welsh Academy and the *Western Mail* for kindly advertising for this tribute. Special thanks to Gethin Gruffudd, Sian Ifan, Meic Stephens and Terry Breverton for their advice and support.

To Gwasg Gomer, the families of Gwenallt and A. G. Prys-Jones, to Dafydd Johnson and Meic Stephens for their kindness and generosity.

To my cousin, Cerys, for her valuable help.

To my father and uncle for passing down to their children our country's songs and stories.

Thanks to Lefi Gruffudd, and his staff at Dinas for their encouragement and enthusiasm in producing this tribute.

And finally, to the poets, past and present. They know why.

Rhys Gruffydd Parry, 2004

Introduction

THIS TRIBUTE TO OWAIN GLYNDŴR is part of the ongoing reclamation of our Welsh history, heritage and culture. Owain ap Gruffudd Fychan ap Gruffudd ap Madog ap Gruffudd Fychan ap Gruffudd ap Madog, Arglwydd Glyndyfrdwy, Lord of Deeside and Sycharth, the heir of King Cadwaladr, is the most renowned of the heroes of Cymru. The English chroniclers of the time recounted his deeds in '*the war of the Welsh against the English*', yet today's trained academics refer to the war of independence from the French incomers as a rebellion.

Thanks to books like Gideon Brough's seminal *Glyn Dŵr's War – The Campaigns of the Last Prince of Wales*, we are uncovering the truth about this truly wonderful and gracious warrior. It seems that he was born upon May 28th, 1354, and died upon September 20th, 1415 at the home of one of his two surviving daughters in Hereford.

With limited resources and voluntary support, Glyndŵr reunited the land against the vastly superior professional forces of the English crown, which were backed by foreign financiers. From his coronation as Prince of Cymru upon September 16th 1400, to the final submission of his supporters at Bala upon March 10th 1414, the nation followed Glyndŵr in his fight against a vicious, illegal regime. These fourteen years saw a dozen English and mercenary armies attack Wales, in six separate invasions, led by the King of England in person. Time and time again they were beaten back in disarray.

In *Henry IV Part I* we hear Glyndŵr pronouncing:

'*Three times hath Henry Bolignbroke made head*

Against my power. Thrice from the banks of the Wye
And sandy-bottomed Severn have I sent
Him bootless home, and weather-beaten back'

Owain was our '*mab darogan*', the son of prophecy of the bards, sent to regain Welsh freedom. The previous mab darogan, Owain Lawgoch, the surviving heir of the princes of Gwynedd, had been assassinated in France in 1378 at Mortagne-sur-Gironde, on the orders of the Franco-English crown. The rest of the family had been extinguished by a process of ritual genocide by the English crown following the treacherous murder of the last Prince of Gwynedd, Llywelyn II.

And it was treachery by the Norman Earl Grey of Ruthin that kindled this war of freedom. The history of Welsh relations with the Normans had been one of one-sided cruelty and evil, which non-coincidentally marked their progress across the rest of Europe. Anglo-Saxon England had fallen immediately to the Norman conquest, but its illiterate rulers never properly conquered Wales until the killing of Llywelyn II, over 200 years later. From then on the country smouldered with resentment until at last Owain threw off the yoke of serfdom.

Under Owain the nation was free again. It is the greatest measure of the pride of the people that he was never betrayed to the English from the time of his disappearance 1414. Not for Owain the ritual hanging, drawing and disembowelling that happened to Llywelyn II's brother Prince Dafydd. Owain Glyndŵr gives our nation memories of independence, culture, bravery and leadership.

But what was left to Owain in 1414? His mansions Glyndyfrdwy and Sycharth had been torched and his estates destroyed. His faithful lieutenants Rhys Ddu, Rhys ap Llywelyn, Rhys Gethin and Phillip Scudamore had been captured and tortured to death. Owain's wife

Marged died in the Tower with two of his daughters and three grand-daughters. His only known grandson, Lionel, the child of Edmund Mortimer and Owain's daughter Catrin, had an excellent claim to the English crown, and was killed. Owain's son Gruffudd died in disgusting conditions in prison. His brother Tudur died in the Battle of Pwll Melin. His son-in-law Mortimer had died at the siege of Harlech. All Owain had left was one son, Maredudd, who finally accepted the King's pardon upon April 8th, 1421, twenty-one years after the war broke out. Owain never accepted a pardon from the Plantagenets. A pardon for what? For fighting for right? For giving his nation everlasting pride?

Our greatest hero, Owain was a noble, cultured warrior feted by Shakespeare as *'not in the roll of common men'*, and as:

> *'a worthy gentlemen,*
> *Exceeding well read, and profited*
> *In strange concealments, valiant as a lion,*
> *And wondrous affable, and as bountiful*
> *As mines in India.'*

The noted historian G. M. Trevelyan called Glyndŵr *'this wonderful man, an attractive and unique figure in a period of debased and selfish politics.'* Even today, he seems to be more highly regarded outside Wales than in it, probably because the Welsh people are not taught their history, heritage and culture in school. British, i.e. Welsh history was debased by the rewriting of British history to begin with the arrival of the Saxons, Jutes and Angles. This Germanification of the facts was carried out by Bishop Stubbs to glorify the achievements of the Hanovers when they took over the Empire by a fluke of birth. Coming from a country the size of the Isle of Wight, the new kings needed justification for their rule, and Welsh-British history was ignored. Ever since, so-called academics have repeated the teachings of their masters.

However, it seems that outside Britain, Glyndŵr is better known. A 1999 Sunday Times survey of 100 world leaders, artists and scientists, including Clinton and Yeltsin, asked for the names of the most significant figures of the last 1000 years.

After Gutenburg, Shakespeare, Leonardo da Vinci, Elizabeth Tudor and Faraday, in 7th place, was Owain Glyndŵr. The fact that the world's great men place him above Einstein, Churchill, Mandela, Bill Gates and Darwin show his importance. There is an air of renaissance in Wales – it is only fitting that the undefeated Glyndŵr should lead us into the 21st century.

Terry Breverton
2004

Llywelyn
ap Gruffydd Fychan*

We come, Llywelyn ap Gruffydd Fychan★,
with our softened hands and the illusion
of a government we can call our own,
to piece back the pieces and rediscover you
whole, memory twining again with desire
to seed, against all common sense, the practical dream.

A day in October (I do not want to see it),
a day maybe of mountain rain, or a day perhaps
like the days you led the king and his lumbering army
up and down and round and round bewildering Deheubarth,
that your sons and Glyndŵr and the nation you were daring
might live to struggle a day, a week, six hundred years longer.
Or an autumn day (I do not want to see it)
as drowsy as a wasp at the gate of an apple, a perfect day
for an execution (I do not want to accept
the usurper king's unkind invitation).
War war war, sle sle sle the Welsh doggis and their whelps.
 I do not want to witness the old father
bound, pistol-whipped and dragged to the gallows,
my eyes resist the advertised spectacle and main attraction
of that pale and pendulous bon viveur's belly
knived at raggedly by the slaughterman's blade
till a gaping smile gives birth vomitous to oodling

screams unanimaled of earth, screams beyond
imagination's hearing, as men tickle, with talons of fire,
the steaming, soft machinery of his being.

Pour encourager les autres. The Empire starts here.
A good thrashing first - then, in the fullness of imperial time,
great kindness: bibles, railways, schools, TV …
I do not want to see on the news
the piked head, the torso loved of woman
quartered, salted, despatched as a warning to the four corners.

And what are we to make of the news?
Who the hero, who the villain? Is not war
a mutual atrocity? And were not the *uchelwyr*,
like as not, hawks and leeches on the lives beneath them?
If this man was loved, was he not rich?
And if rich Cymru's rich in hope in a ravened world
who is it, out of mind, that pays the price?

What we have made of the news is not what the king
would have us make, and we come, Llywelyn,
to piece back the pieces, to conjure home
your hatcheted limbs, to restore to those shoulders
your hazarding head and trickster smile, to wind those
blasphemed lights back within sound of your heart's *llan* -
and then in your right, unwavering hand
to settle a beaker of Gascony wine.

Your house, Llywelyn, is today a hill, and out of that hill
an oak rears, seismic with acorns: timber for ships, barrels, dreams –
for the hall you left us that's ours to complete.

Nigel Jenkins

* Llywelyn ap Gruffydd Fychan, of Caeo in Carmarthenshire, was a
prosperous landowner and supporter of Owain Glyndŵr who was
press-ganged by Henry IV into helping him find Glyndŵr's base.
Llywelyn led Henry and his army on a wild goose chase, enabling
Owain to escape to Gwynedd. Realizing that he had been duped,
Henry had Llywelyn publicly disembowelled and dismembered in
front of the castle gates at Llanymddyfri on October 9, 1401. This
poem was commissioned for the unveiling of a memorial to
Llywelyn at Llanymddyfri on October 6, 2001.

GLYNDŴR ROAD

No way through Glyndŵr Road –
blocked by the Drill Hall
(still scuffed by marks
of a deathwatch tattoo)

Where are the sons & daughters now?
The curved arrows on cars
tell they're living
in unassuming terraces –
of C for Cymraeg
of a Celtic curve
of a red dragon's tongue

but EUROPE IS MY NATION
rebels against the rebellion –
as if, 'Aber is my city'
when all says smalltown

Will they leave and climb
the followers of the sign?
How soon will commoners become
the newfound noblemen?

Glyndŵr Road leads to itself –

but time will come
when they will turn
their backs on the Drill Hall
(pink as Empire)
and move away
beyond sea   beyond mountains
towards a high-walled skyline
and down
into the city they can never
call home.

Mike Jenkins

Rhyfela hyd farw

Boed i Gymru ail-gofio y dyddiau fu
Cyn i'w meibion ei bradychu,
Pan arweiniai Owain ei wlatgar lu
Cyn i ysbryd y dewrion nychu,
Pan ddisgleiriai ein harfau ar fynydd a chraig,
Pan atseiniai banllef Garmon,
A bu'r heulwen yn gwenu ar Faner y Ddraig
Cyn i fagddu caethiwed ddod arnom.

Ar ol oesoedd tywyllwch yng ngharchar y Sais
Yn awr daw ein cyfle i godi,
Daw diwrnod rhyddhad o gadwyni trais
Bydd y gelyn yn cael ei ddifodi,
Tyngwn lw i ail-adfer holl freintiau ein gwlad
Er bod llwybrau anrhydedd yn arw,
Ac er gwaethaf pob cynllwyn a dichell a brâd
Tyngwn lw i ryfela hyd farw.

Harri Webb

By a mountain pool

Now by this sulky mountain pool I pause.
Its waters are as dark and deep a blue
As if it were the sea, but it is shallow,
A gathering of rains, a sheep pond only,
Yet, even in the mist, ultramarine
As deep and dark as if it were the sea.
Is this my country's image? Have I leapt
Into a fancied ocean, sink or swim,
Only to stumble in a shallow pool
And suffocate in mud? Yet even now
The water is so blue it seems a jewel
Lost by a god here on the high wet moors.
Be you my mirror, lakelet of the mountains,
Now as I raise my wearied hands to lift
The heavy dragon helmet from my shoulders
For the last time.
      It was not always so.
A plain steel helmet hastily adorned
With Corwen smith-work was my only crown
When those lads rode with me from Glyndyfrdwy
Up to the Clwydian hills and made me king.
And when the land was ours they gave me a crown
Of fine French jewelry, and this great dragon helm
To guard that crown, the golden crown of Wales.
And when I drove the English from the land

And seemed to command the lightning and the thunder,
And when my star burned over burning castles,
Then was the hour of the dragon, my blazing crest.
And in the long retreat from the fickle south,
The bargaining west, the supine central valleys,
The steadfast men who carried in their swords
The soul of Wales kept their eyes on the dragon
And held their heads up proudly as they rode
With Owain into the mist, where now I wander,
An old man, alone by a mountain pool,
The mirror of an ageing face, white hair
That shone red-gold in the breeze of the Clwydian hills
When I was crowned with steel.
                    For all too long
I have looked out on the world through helmet bars,
My voice has echoed iron in command
Out from the faceless helm, even to myself
An iron voice, echoing inside my skull.
But now the iron echoes die away;
Unhelmeted, I see my face in the pool
With no bars in between, no dragon crest
Ramping implacably above my head,
An old man's face, seen in a mountain pool,
And every furrow of age and scar of battle
The dark water deepens, and my eyes
Are shadow, bottomless shadow that goes down
Deeper than the water that reflects them.
The great helm here in the crook of my arm
At last now bears too heavy for my age,

A thing of rusted steel and faded crest
That should hang honourably in an old man's hall
And hang at last in church over his tomb.
But I can have no certain resting place
And Owain's grave must always be unknown.
The hall is not yet built, the church not hallowed
That dares to house the royalty of Wales.
This pool's the place, no shepherd wandering here,
No anxious traveller, no hastening drover
Will ever spare a glance or a stray thought
For this blue scrap of water. Only the flocks
And waterfowl will trouble it at the edge
And never know what greatness is drowned here.
It is best so. All strife, all hope is drowned.
I give it to the keeping of the mountains,
I give it to the keeping of the waters.
I quench the heraldry of sovereign Wales
Here in this pool. So. It is gone. It is done.
The dragon's fire is out. Now I ride home
Bareheaded, the wet mist beading my hair.
And as the iron echoes die away
The wind stirs in the mist and in the wind–
Voices.
      Owain!
        Voices, voices I hear
From nowhere.
      From afar.
          This cannot be.
I wore the great helmet too long, the echoing iron,

And am haunted now by echoes of old voices
Out of the past.

Out of the future, Owain.
We speak from the unbuilt cities, from a time unborn,
From beyond experience, beyond imagination.

You speak to mock me, an old broken man.
But no, these are not fiends' voices. Blazon yourselves,
Your names, your nation and your quality.

It is enough that you should know our nation.
Our names are a ragman roll and our quality
No better, but our nation is your nation.

It lives beyond this darkness? Beyond the ruin
Of town and farm? Beyond the death I made?

Because you made this death the nation lives.

After this dark night, there came a dawn?

After this dark night there came a darker,
And darkness on darkness and then a long dawn,
A struggling sickly dawn as long as the darkness.

But where you speak from, does the sun now shine?

We have caught at last a glimpse of the red sun
And its redness is the colour of the dragon

Drowned by a fugitive prince in a moorland pool.

How are you mustered? What is your armament?
What bards sing you to battle? What allies?

Our friends are few and hard-pressed as ourselves.
Our strength is our own, none other and none the worse.

I know you are indeed my nation. Speak on.

Beyond the darkness: beyond the mists of morning,
By the farthest shore and in the inmost valleys,
We muster to your summons and to the call
Of all the other captains of our people
From those first swords that lit the fires of dawn
When we held out against the brazen eagles
From the hot south and from the hungry north
The harsh black ravens to that weary day
That falls to us, the day of the drab vultures,
The carrion breed of Mersey and of Thames,
The living dead, the songless bringers of silence.
We send our message to you across time
That is halted forever in the heart of our wild hills,
To you alone by a mountain pool in the mist
From the cities of neon and nylon, the glass battlements,
From a land besieged, seduced by alien witchcraft,
Against a taller terror than ever strode
In armour through the woods or beached the longships,
A sly assault of black legality

That wears no blazoned baldric nor horned hat
But brings a surer death than ever their swords.

He too I had to face. At Croesau Common
My proud neighbour, Grey of Ruthun, invoked him
And sent me home insulted from his court.
But I burnt Ruthun and I beggared Grey.
And more than Croesau Common were in the balance,
But all the lands of Wales, was it ours or theirs?
But I was a young man then. Now I am old and finished.
Leave me in peace. Why do you call on me?
I failed.

It is not we who call on you
But you on us, that we must keep faith with Owain
Or die shamed.

I drowned it, I tell you, here in the mist.
In a mountain pool I drowned my faith and my kingdom.
They are gone like water. Let the water keep them.
How can they rise again?

They rise again from the water,
From all the waters of Wales, from all the rivers,
Her torrent brooks, her lakes, her mountain pools.
Where the mist rises at evening or dawn
The warriors ride again along the valleys:
Wherever water speaks by a bridge in the twilight
Or whispers on gravel at noon, it is a voice

That hisses shame on those who keep no faith,
It is a voice that never can be silenced.
It is your voice, Owain.

I give you my voice again:
Fight on. You have kept faith with me, I will
Keep faith with you. Wherever you strike in vengeance
My strength is in your arm. You have come to me
In a chill twilight, from deep in the pool of the sleep
Of the dragon.

That does not sleep.

You have come to call me
To the battle I had thought ended when the last
Blow was struck on the banks of Monmouth river.

Owain, the rivers of Wales are numberless
And every river a battle, and every battle a song.
Our bards shall string their harps with battles and rivers
And you shall ride with us, fording them one by one
As we take them, one by one, back into our keeping.

Harri Webb

the Red, white and green

On the first day of March we remember
St. David the pride of our land,
Who taught us the stern path of duty
And for freedom and truth made a stand.

So here's to the sons of Saint David,
Those youngsters so loyal and keen
Who'll haul down the red, white and blue, lads,
And hoist up the red, white and green.

In the dark gloomy days of December
We mourn for Llywelyn with pride
Who fell in defence of his country
With eighteen brave men by his side.

So here's to the sons of Llywelyn,
The heirs of that valiant eighteen
Who'll haul down the red, white and blue, lads,
And hoist up the red, white and green.

In the warm, golden days of September,
Great Owain Glyndŵr took the field,
For fifteen long years did he struggle
And never the dragon did yield.

So here's to the sons of Great Owain,
Who'll show the proud Sais what we mean
When we haul down the red, white and blue, lads,
And hoist up the red, white and green.

There are many more names to remember
And some that will never be known
Who were loyal to Wales and the gwerin
And defied all the might of the throne.

So here's to sons of the gwerin
Who care not for prince or for queen,
Who'll haul down the red, white and blue, lads,
And hoist up the red, white and green!

Harri Webb

Owain Glyndŵr

The harps are all silent, the flags are all furled,
And darkness has covered the face of the world.
From valley to valley the whisper has flown
That dead is Prince Owain and empty his throne.
For fifteen long winters the struggle he bore
For freedom and justice, but now it's all o'er.
    Sleep soundly, brave Owain, though battle was vain,
    The time may well come when we'll call you again.

Like the shadows of clouds and the green hills of Wales
The centuries pass, but still linger the tales
Of a prince who rode foremost in Cymru's just fight,
And brought a proud nation from darkness to light.
For him the rains weep and the winter winds moan,
But the grave of our hero's for ever unknown.
    Sleep soundly, brave Owain, your time is not yet,
    But your fight for our freedom no man will forget.

The centuries have passed but the battle's not done,
And the cause that he died for has yet to be won,
With his memory to stir us, his deeds to inflame,
We will conquer our freedom in Owain's great name,
Strike hard at the traitors and cleanse all the land
With the keen sword of vengeance we take from his hand.
    Our country is calling, we strive for her sake,
    Sleep soundly, Prince Owain, your sons are awake!

Harri Webb

the Rising of Glyndŵr

Thunder-browed and shaggy-throated
All the men were there,
And the women with the hair
That is the raven's and the rook's despair.

Winds awoke, and vixen-footed
Firelight prowled the glade ;
The stars were hooded and the moon afraid
To vex the darkness with her yellow braid.

Then he spoke, and anger kindled
In each brooding eye ;
Swords and spears accused the sky,
The woods resounded with a bitter cry.

Beasts gave tongue and barn-howls hooted,
Every branch grew loud
With the menace of that crowd,
That thronged the dark, huge as a thundercloud.

R. S. Thomas

hyddgen

The place, Hyddgen ;
The time, the fifth
Century since Glyn Dŵr
Was here with his men.
He beat the English.
Does it matter now
In the rain ? The English
Don't want to come :
Summer country.
The Welsh too :
A barren victory.
Look at those sheep,
On such small bones
The best mutton,
But not for him,
The hireling shepherd.
History goes on ;
On the rock the lichen
Records it : no mention
Of them, of us.

R. S. Thomas

the tree

Owain Glyn Dŵr speaks

Gruffudd Llwyd put into my head
The strange thought, singing of the dead
In *awdl* and *cywydd* to the harp,
As though he plucked with each string
The taut fibres of my being.
Accustomed to Iolo and his praise
Of Sycharth with its brown beer,
Meat from the chase, fish from the weir,
Its proud women sipping wine,
I had equated the glib bards
With flattery and the expected phrase,
Tedious concomitants of power.
But Gruffudd Llwyd with his theme
Of old princes in whose veins
Swelled the same blood that sweetened mine
Pierced my lethargy, I heard
Above the tuneful consonants
The sharp anguish, the despair
Of men beyond my smooth domain
Fretting under the barbed sting
Of English law, starving among
The sleek woods no longer theirs.
And I remembered that old nurse
Prating of omens in the sky

When I was born, the heavens inflamed
With meteors and the stars awry.
I shunned the thought, there was the claim
Of wife and young ones, my first care,
And Sycharth, too ; I would dismiss
Gruffudd. But something in his song
Stopped me, held me ; the bright harp
Was strung with fire, the music burned
All but the one green thought away.
The thought grew to a great tree
In the full spring time of the year ;
The far tribes rallied to its green
Banner waving in the wind ;
Its roots were nourished with their blood.
And days were fair under those boughs ;
The dawn foray, the dusk carouse
Bred the stout limb and blither heart
That marked us of Llywelyn's brood.
It was with us as with the great ;
For one brief hour the summer came
To the tree's branches and we heard
In the green shade Rhiannon's birds
Singing tirelessly as the streams
That pluck glad tunes from the grey stones
Of Powys of the broken hills.

The music ceased, the obnoxious wind
And frost of autumn picked the leaves
One by one from the gaunt boughs ;

They fell, some in a gold shower
About its roots, but some were hurled
Out of my sight, out of my power,
Over the face of the grim world.

It is winter still in the bare tree
That sprang from the seed which Gruffudd sowed
In my hot brain in the long nights
Of wine and music on the hearth
Of Sycharth of the open gates.
But here at its roots I watch and wait
For the new spring so long delayed ;
And he who stands in the light above
And sets his ear to the scarred bole,
Shall hear me tell from the deep tomb
How sorrow may bud the tree with tears,
But only his blood can make it bloom.

R. S. Thomas

A Ballad of Glyndŵr's Rising

I

My son, the moon is crimson, and a mist is in the sky:
Oh can't you hear the thudding feet, the horsemen
    speeding by?
Oh can't you hear the muttering that swells upon the breeze,
And the whispers that are stealing through the chancel of
    the trees?
To-night we two go riding, for the threads of fate are spun,
And we muster far at Corwen at the rising of the sun.

II

My son, the winds are calling, and the mountains and
    the flood
With a wail of deep oppression that wakes havoc in my
    blood.
And I have waited, waited long throughout the bitter years
For this hour of freedom's challenge and the flashing of
    the spears:
So we two go riding, riding, through the meshes of the night,
That we hail Glyndŵr at Corwen at the breaking of the light.

III

My son, go kiss your mother, kiss her gently, she'll not
  wake,
For a greater mother calls you, though you perish for her
  sake:
Lo! the Dragon flag is floating out across the silver Dee,
And the soul of Wales is crying at the very heart of me-
Crying justice, crying vengeance: pray, my son, for strength
  anew,
For there's many will be sleeping at the falling of the dew.

A. G. Prys-Jones

Rebirth

Driven from unnatural duty
By the evil shade of grey
From moated mansion at Sycharth
And plas at Glyndyfrdwy
Owain regained the nationhood –
Our candle of battle

In spring the blood-poured lions of Gwynedd roared
In summer the men of Cymru unsheathed their swords
In Autumn the invasions became stronger
And winter fell upon the nation

6 centuries of loss
20 generations of despair
60 decades of Trywerin
600 years of Aberfan

The invisible immortal
The defender of our nation
Never betrayed –
Still shelters his blasted people
Ever present but unseen

Born in Spring
Lived out Summer
Died in Autumn
Without Winter
As yet
There is no Spring

Terry Breverton

nationalism

"The Welsh people are now nothing but a naked people under an acid rain"
Gwyn Alf Williams, *When Was Wales* (1985)

when you came
in your wars
you called us Walsci
– "foreigners"
in our own lands
– and pushed us to peripheries

you trespass
on our mirrors
of hills and grass

you do not want the history
   so you will repeat the mistakes of the past
you do not want our language
   so your mongreloid tongue conquered the world
      while the Welsh Not was yoked round our
         brightest necks

[I have a cunning plan
Said the Ministry Man
Let's cut out the Tongue
Heart, liver and Lung]

you take our water and you took our coal
and only Japanese arrogance employs our women
......on a pittance
our new imported peasantry, Thatcher's people, agree with you

our laws date from before windows
    [a word borrowed from the Romans]
our laws were the first to believe women's words
our church was socialist

you believe in fate when you run out of chances

our battle honours are Gresford and Aberfan
yours are Ramillies and Agincourt

we are the red kites of Europe
once in the natural centre
then feeding off carrion in the urban sprawl
so pushed out to peripheries
away from the Saesneg and assorted killers
few remain
worrying R. S. Thomas' "dead carcass"
to the lazy ebb and flow of the buzzard's beat of wing

in 2000 years we have never started a war
perhaps it is time

Terry Breverton

in the hill-country

I

Beneath this massy keep
And down this glen
Rode our great lord, the Prince Glyndŵr,
That king of men;
But now the years are old
And his hearths are cold...
And he will not ride again.

II

But yet I saw him come,
Stalwart and strong,
Riding-with eyes that blazed like stars-
To quench a wrong:
And this I saw and heard
In a dream that stirred
Out of a peasant's song.

III

I saw him come once more,
Still proud and tall,
But there were none to staunch his wounds
Or hear his call:

And he passed from grave to grave,
But the dead no answer gave
To his lone footfall.

IV

And so, from hill to hill,
Calling, he crept
Until Death answered, 'Come-my Prince'...
And the woods wept:
And they rode where no man knows-
Not even the wind that blows
Saw where his great soul slept.

A. G. Prys-Jones

the passing
of owain glyndŵr

(Black Mountains, 1416)

Now fades the twilight from the quiet sky,
On cairn and croft the cloaks of darkness fall,
Home to their eyries the great buzzards fly,
And over dusky pools the curlews call:
And here by twisting bridle-paths at night
Came one all travel-stained and battle-torn
Who paused and listened in his friendless plight
To reapers late among the upland corn,
Prince Owain of the Dee, with weary eyes,
Seeking the hills from glen to winding glen
Where the great moors and forests roll and rise,
The refuge of defeated, broken men,
With hounds of Harry Monmouth in full cry
Loosed from the leash where Prince Llywelyn fell,
And listening, he saw the lowland sky
Glow red with flame, and heard his passing-bell.

And here, men say, he vanished in the dawn
Leaving no sigh save a wide-open door,
His baldric and his naked sword forlorn
In some deserted hut below the moor,
Where comforted by mourning rain that wept

For his doomed cause, and lulled by sighing trees,
Through these, his darkest hours, he lay and slept:
And then, awakened by the mountain breeze
He rose and shook aside his poignant pain
And strode away unarmed, still proud and brave:
But no one heard his hero-voice again,
And no man knows where lies his lonely grave.

A. G. Prys-Jones

sycharth

The brittle grass and the fading moon,
I visited Sycharth on a morning born cold,
not even a brief respite of sun
like the yellow of an old bruise
appeared on the skin of day;
inaudible the conversations
once held there,
a ringed mound
where
Iolo's
imagination praised
Glyndŵr's home,
the strong tapestries in his court of plenty,
a fishpond, dovecote, and heronry,
the wine burning the flames of his blood
into poetry, but that day the language froze,
with the curvature of an easterly draught, as uninvited
shadows came to encase this altruistic scenery.

Byron Beynon

parliament house at machynlleth

Near here an alliance was once etched
with France, Glyndŵr's representatives in Europe,
received with courtesy, his seal
on a letter from Wales,
a blueprint in time
requesting military assistance,
preserved now like a distant memory;
a tribe of clouds
chill the modern air
in a market town
kept busy with a minibus of students
parked with clipboards,
elastic locals and visitors passing through
as a senedd of birds take flight,
a surviving arc breaking free
into the changing scenery of ebullient light.

Byron Beynon

A Dried Deer Skin

"Go there and see for yourself", says Mrs Huws as we stand in her farmyard at Rhos-y-Garreg. "Where else but there could the Prince and his boys have camped before the battle?" Siambr Trawsfynydd - The Chamber Across the Mountain - a fold in the hills faithfully recorded by the Ordnance Survey.

From Owain Glyndŵr's website to the site of his first great victory. I reverse the red estate out from under his royal standard, hanging from a rafter in our barn.

> draped with the dusty cobwebs
> of shrivelled spiders
> crimson lions on a field of gold

The dense thickets of ash, birch and dwarf oak, long the haunt of patriots, poets and other outlaws, are now a lonely upland of tussock and sitka spruce. But the steep hills remain, with their bogs and crags, the clear streams and the thin rain. There is still no habitation or road for miles, and to meet a stranger is cause for conversation. "No one who knows this place well will deny that certain things are possible here and nowhere else", observes a sober Victorian gazetteer. Here past and present slide easily over one another. Did not Iorwerth Jones of Aberhosen witness the battle, and celebrate it in the 160 lines of poetry that won him the bardic chair at the Powys Eisteddfod in 1977?

And so, on this misty evening, see, *there* is the Prince himself, tall in his leathers, strolling and conferring with a younger man in clerical garb - surely his secretary, Rhisiart?

> Attention caught
> by their antique cut
> the clothes of ghosts

They take no notice of me.

Hyddgen it is called - a level ground in the folds of the hills like a "deer skin" stretched out to dry. Owain's "one hundred and twenty reckless men and robbers" lie nearby, concealed in the shallow wooded ravines:

> Woodsmoke and mist
> the cooking fires
> of dead men

1401, an hour before dawn, late in the month of May, fifteen hundred men in heavy gear are slogging it up the mountain. Here are the Flemish settlers, planted in Pembrokeshire by an English king, cursing Owain for his winter raiding. At the head of the column are the English men-at arms commanded by John Charlton, lord of Powys. Head down, the veteran recalls the centuries of struggle against the Welsh, the steep tangled country, the vile weather.

Armour streaked with rust
and at the ford
a shower of arrows

And now there's this Glendourdy, shape-shifting wizard and
conjuror of storms.

Stealthily Charlton's men fan out around the rebel camp.

By waters flowing
over blood red lichens
the crouching shadows

The folds in the hills are filled with mist. Stillness before dawn. And
then, for one of Owain's sentinels,

In the silence
of an empty land
faint clink
of iron

Their backs to Llechwedd Diflas – Hill of Despair – the Welsh fight
like demons. Thrusting, hacking, – men butcher men. Their foemen
falter, fall back, turn, and flee. With the rout comes the greatest
slaughter.

Today the Nant Goch lies hidden deep in forestry:

> Red River —
> running headlong
> through bleached and broken pines

"And thus did Owain win great fame, and a great number of youths and fighting men from every part of Wales rose and joined him, until he had a great host at his back."

Ken Jones

sycharth

The grove of Sycharth

                       is still today,

the streamlet of Cynllaith

             progresses

at a slow pace

            and the ancient bridge

            which receives the brook,

once held

        our noble Prince of Powys

adorned

       in gold.

A grassy mound

                enclosed by a barren moat

are all that remains

         of the "mansion to the clouds,"

a silhouette

         that occupies the consciousness

of the onlooker

       as he embraces

the spirit

     of the

       Cambrian knight.

Welsh people

                    lived close to sorrow
but Glyndŵr's flame
                    burnt brighter
the deeper
the darkness spread
                    and though the Saxon bigotry
was savage
            in its malevolence
the sword
                was drawn
                        and the
standard raised.

Dusk
        encroaches
                and owls break the silence
with their melody,
                Sycharth·
                        unpretentious
and desolate
            abides serenely
against
            the horizon.

The
halls
of gold
            are long gone

        though decay

will not dishonour it;

and time will not touch it;

        for it remains a sacred

        site,

the land of Glyndŵr

with its fields of freedom

        and visions of independence

living

in the heart

of every

Welshman.

Alan Wyke

achau owain glyndŵr

Myfyrio bûm i farwn
Moliant dyhuddiant i hwn;
Arwyrain Owain a wnaf,
Ar eiriau mydr yr euraf
Peunydd, nid naddiad gwŷdd gwern,
Pensaerwawd paun y Sirwern.
Pwy yng nghlawr holl Faelawr hir,
Paun, rhwy Glyndyfrdwy dyfrdir,
Pwy a ddylai, ped fai fyd,
- Pwy ond Owain, paun diwyd? -
Y ddwy Faelawr mawr eu mâl,
Eithr efo, a Mathrafal?
Pwy a ostwng Powystir,
Pe bai gyfraith a gwaith gwir?
Pwy eithr y mab penaethryw,
Owain Gruffudd, Nudd in yw,
Fab Gruffudd, llafnrudd yw'r llall,
Gryfgorff gymen ddigrifgall,
Orwyr Madog, iôr medeingl,
Fychan yn ymseingian Eingl,
Goresgynnydd Ruffudd rwydd
Maelawr, gywirglawr arglwydd,
Hil Fadog hiroediog hen,
Gymro ger hoywfro Hafren,
Hwyliwr yr holl Ddeheuwlad,

Hil Arglwydd Rhys, gwŷs i gad,
Hil Fleddyn, hil Gynfyn gynt,
Hil Aedd, o ryw hael oeddynt,
Hil Faredudd rudd ei rôn,
Tëyrn Carneddau Teon,
Hil y Gwinau Dau Freuddwyd,
Hil Bywer Lew, fy llew llwyd,
Hil Ednyfed, lifed lafn,
Hil Uchdryd lwyd, hael wychdrafn,
Hil Dewdwr mawr, gwawr gwerin,
Heliwr â gweilch, heiliwr gwin,
Hil Faig Mygrfras, gwas gwaywsyth,
Heirdd fydd ei feirdd o'i fodd fyth.
Hawddamor pôr eurddor pert,
Hwyl racw ym mrwydr, hil Ricert,
Barwn mi a wn ei ach,
Ni bu barwn bybyrach;
Anoberi un barwn
Eithr y rhyw yr henyw hwn.
Gorwyr, dioer, o gaer Dwyrain,
Gwenllian o Gynan gain.
Medd y ddwy Wynedd einym,
Da yw, a gatwo Duw ym,
Wrth bawb ei ortho a'i bwyll,
Arth o Ddeheubarth hoywbwyll,
Cynyddwr pobl cyneiddwng,
Cnyw blaidd ydyw'r cenau blwng,
Balch a dewr, bylchai darian,
Beli y Glyn, bual glân,

Llew Prydain, llaw Peredur,
Llew siaced tew soced dur,
Pestel cad, arglwydd-dad glew,
Post ardal Lloegr, pais durdew,
Edling o hen genhedlaeth
Yw ef o ben Tref y Traeth;
Ei gyfoeth, ef a'i gofyn,
Tref y Garn, a'i farn a fyn;
Gwrthrych fydd, gorthrech ei farn,
Gwrthrychiad gorthir Acharn.
Mab da arab dihaereb
Hyd hyn fu, ni wybu neb;
Gŵr bellach a grybwyllir,
Ni wneir dwyn un erw o'i dir;
Marchog ffyrf rhieddog rhwydd,
Mawrchwyrn lle bu'r ymorchwydd;
Neur aeth, asgwrn nerth esgud,
Ei floedd, o'i droed mae'n flaidd drud.
Garw wrth arw, gŵr wrth eraill,
Ufudd a llonydd i'r llaill,
Llonydd wrth wan, rhan ei raid,
Aflonydd I fileiniaid.
Llew Is Coed, lluosog ged,
Llaw a wna llu eniwed,
Llithio'r brain, llethu Brynaich
Â llath bren mwy na llwyth braich.
Be magwn, byw ymogor,
Genau i neb, egin iôr,
Hael eurddrem, hwyl awyrddraig,

I hwn y magwn, ail Maig.
Tawwn, gorau yw tewi,
Am hwn ni ynganwn ni;
Da daint rhag tafod, daw dydd,
Yng nghilfach safn anghelfydd,
Cael o hwn, coel a honnir,
Calon Is Aeron a'i sir,
Ac iechyd a phlant gwycheirdd
Yn Sycharth, buarth y beirdd.
Corwen, Dyfrdwy, Conwy, Cain,
Cai fath hoyw, cyfoeth Owain;
Un gad, un llygad, un llaw,
Aur burffrwyth iôr Aberffraw;
Un pen ar Gymru, wen wedd,
Ac un enaid gan Wynedd,
Un llygad, cymyniad caith,
Ac unllaw yw i Gynllaith.

Iolo Goch

moliant owain glyndŵr

Mawr o symud a hud hydr
A welwn ni ar welydr.
Archwn i Fair, arch iawn fu,
Noddi'r bual gwineuddu,
Arglwydd terwyn o'r Glyn glwys
Yw'r Pywer Lew, iôr Powys.
Pwy adwaenai bai'n y byd,
Pwy ond Owain, paun diwyd?
Rhwysg y iarll balch gwyarllwybr,
Rhysgyr mab Llŷr ym mhob llwybr.
Anoberi un barwn
Ond y rhyw yr henyw hwn;
Hynod yw henw ei daid,
Brenin ar y barwniaid;
Ei dad, pawb a wyddiad pwy,
Iôr Glyn, daeardor, Dyfrdwy;
Hiriell, Cymru ddihaereb,
Oedd ei dad yn anad neb;
Pwy bynnag fo'r Cymro call,
Bythorud? – gwn beth arall;
Gorau mab rhwng gŵr a mam
O Bowys, foddlwys fuddlam;
Os mab, mab yn adnabod
Caru clêr, felly ceir clod.
Ni fyn i un ofyn ach

I feibion, ni bu fwbach;
Ni ddug degan o'i anfodd
Gan fab ond a gâi o'i fodd;
Ni pheris drwy gis neu gur
Iddo â'i ddwylo ddolur;
Ni chamodd fys na chymwyll
Cymain' â bw, cymen bwyll.

Pan aeth mewn gwroliaeth gwrdd,
Gorugwr fu garw agwrdd,
Ni wnaeth ond marchogaeth meirch,
Gorau amser, mewn gwrmseirch,
Dwyn paladr, gwaladr gwiwlew,
Soced dur a siaced tew,
Arwain rhest a phenffestin
A helm wen, gŵr hael am win,
Ac yn ei phen, nen iawnraifft,
Adain rudd o edn yr Aifft.
Gorau sawdwr gwrs ydoedd
Gyda Syr Grigor, iôr oedd,
Ym Merwig, hirdrig herwdref,
Maer i gadw'r gaer gydag ef.
Gair mawr am fwrw y gŵr march
A gafas pan fu gyfarch,
A'i gwympio yno'n gampus
I lawr, a'i aesawr yn us.
A'r ail grwydr a fu brwydr brid,
A dryll ei wayw o drallid;

Cof a chyfliw heddiw hyn,
Cannwyll brwydr, can holl Brydyn;
Rhai'n llefain, rhai'n druain draw,
Pob drygddyn, pawb dioer rhagddaw
Yn gweiddi megis gwyddeifr,
Gyrrodd ofn, garw fu i Ddeifr.
Mawr fu y llwybr drwy'r crwybr crau,
Blwyddyn yn porthi bleiddiau;
Ni thyfodd gwellt na thafol
Hefyd na'r ŷd ar ei ôl,
O Ferwig Seisnig ei sail
Hyd Faesbwrch, hydr fu ysbail.

Iolo Goch

Llys Owain Glyndŵr

Addewais hyd hyn ddwywaith,
Addewid teg, addo taith;
Taled bawb, tâl hyd y bo,
Ei addewid a addawo.
Pererindawd, ffawd ffyddlawn,
Perwyl mor annwyl, mawr iawn,
Myned, eidduned oddáin,
Lles yw, tua llys Owain;
Yn oddáin yno ydd af,
Nid drwg, yno y trigaf
I gymryd i'm bywyd barch
Gydag ef o gydgyfarch;
Fo all fy naf, uchaf ach,
Eurben clear, erbyn cleiriach;
Clod bod, cyd boed alusen,
Ddiwarth hwyl, yn dda wrth hen.
I'w lys ar ddyfrys ydd af,
O'r deucant odidocaf.
Llys barwn, lle syberwyd,
Lle daw beirdd aml, lle da byd;
Gwawr Bowys fawr, beues Faig,
Gofuned gwiw ofynaig.

Llyna'r modd a'r llun y mae
Mewn eurgylch dwfr mewn argae:

(Pand da'r llys?) pont ar y llyn,
Ac unporth lle'r ai ganpyn;
Cyplau sydd, gwaith cwplws ŷnt,
Cwpledig pob cwpl ydynt;
Clochdy Padrig, Ffrengig ffrwyth,
Clostr Wesmustr, clostir esmwyth;
Cynglynrhwym pob congl unrhyw,
Cangell aur, cyngan oll yw;
Cynglynion yn fronfron fry,
Dordor megis daeardy,
A phob un fal llun llyngwlm
Sydd yn ei gilydd yn gwlm;
Tai nawplad fold deunawplas,
Tai pren glân mewn top bryn glas;
Ar bedwar piler eres
Mae'i lys ef i nef yn nes;
Ar ben pob piler pren praff
Llofft ar dalgrofft adeilgraff,
A'r pedair llofft o hoffter
Yn gydgwplws lle cwsg clêr;
Aeth y pedair disgleirlofft,
Nyth lwyth teg iawn, yn wyth lofft;
To teils ar bob tŷ talwg,
A simnai lle magai'r mwg;
Naw neuadd gyfladd gyflun,
A naw gwardrob ar bob un,
Siopau glân glwys cynnwys cain,
Siop lawndeg fal Siêp Lundain;
Croes eglwys gylchlwys galchliw,

Capelau â gwydrau gwiw;
Popty llawn poptu i'r llys,
Perllan, gwinllan ger gwenllys;
Melin deg ar ddifreg ddŵr,
A'i glomendy gloyw maendwr;
Pysgodlyn, cudduglyn cau,
A fo rhaid i fwrw rhwydau;
Amlaf lle, nid er ymliw,
Penhwyaid a gwyniaid gwiw,
A'i dir bwrdd a'i adar byw,
Peunod, crehyrod hoywryw;
Dolydd glân gwyran a gwair,
Ydau mewn caeau cywair,
Parc cwning ein pôr cenedl,
Erydr a meirch hyder, mawr chwedl;
Gerllaw'r llys, gorlliwio'r llall,
Y pawr ceirw mewn parc arall;
Ei gaith a wna pob gwaith gwiw,
Cyfreidiau cyfar ydiw,
Dwyn blaendrwyth cwrw Amwythig,
Gwirodau bragodau brig,
Pob llyn, bara gwyn a gwin,
A'i gig a'i dân i'w gegin;
Pebyll y beirdd, pawb lle bo,
Pe beunydd, caiff pawb yno;
Tecaf llys bren, pen heb bai,
O'r deyrnas, nawdd Duw arnai;
A gwraig orau o'r gwragedd,
Gwyn fy myd o'i gwin a'i medd!

Merch eglur llin marchoglyw,
Urddol hael anianol yw;
A'i blant a ddeuant bob ddau,
Nythiad teg o benaethau.
Anfynych iawn fu yno
Weled na chliced na chlo,
Na phorthoriaeth ni wnaeth neb;
Ni bydd eisiau, budd oseb,
Na gwall na newyn na gwarth,
Na syched fyth yn Sycharth.
Gorau Cymro, tro trylew,
Piau'r wlad, lin Pywer Lew,
Gŵr meingryf, gorau mangre,
A phiau'r llys, hoff yw'r lle.

Iolo Goch

catrin glyndŵr

[a gipiwyd i'r Tŵr, yn Llundain a'i charcharu yno]

Wedi'r brad ar baradwys,
      a'i dwyn yn yr oriau dwys
O'r fan a fu yn annedd.

Bu dur amdani'n furiau,
      mewn gwlad bell a'r gell ar gau –
yn anair, bu'n ddienw.

Bu'n wâr wrth hirymaros
      yn oriau noeth hwyra'r nos,
bu'n anian pob hunaniaeth.

Er hanes blin ddrycinoedd,
      bu'n rhiain gywrain ar goedd,
yn cadw urddas traserch.

Wrth y mur deil aberth merch
      I hawlio'r gri i wylo'r gred:
'Hi hen eleni ganed.'

Menna Elfyn

the exile's song

Betrayal in paradise
       taken in the dark hours
from the place that was home.

Irons like walls around her
       In a distant land her cell locked
wordless, nameless.

Courteous in her long waiting
       in the naked late night hours
her soul, her whole identity.

Despite her stormy history of sorrow
       in public she was the finest maiden
keeping her dignity for the power of love

By the wall, a woman's sacrifice
       upholds the cry, faith's tears
'She old, born again.'

**Translated from the Welsh of Menna Elfyn
by Gillian Clarke**

Glyndŵr Subdued

Burned out, there was no road back,
and the flames of Sycharth brought Glyndŵr
dreams enough:
his home was a country now,
the revenges multiplied.
The helicopter's shadow,
a great hare
runs fleetingly across a field –
the grass panicking, flattened,
trying to disperse but unable.

Almost an experiment,
the disciplined ructions of the first raid,
the strained respect for brawny lives
a delicate line: Rhuthun settlers,

robbed and dishevelled, emerged
to a heady, bright, small Welsh triumph
reeking of sheepshit
and soot in the bright sun:

insults counted, it was a homely,
small, scared, village altercation
as shoving and grunting skirmishes
around slag once made history.

The victors clattered away
shod heavily with expensive curses
to where even the sparks on the hill
were drunk down by the mud and the dark.

Later the conscripts, cast-off and dangerous,
sported their rusted dream of omnipotence,
hacking for their neglected fields
and their friends cut down,

and then for the riven cold in their bones
women ran in the wet grass
brought down like deer with cries of triumph.
People ran blindly,

made his, the pervasive guerilla
reeking of smoke and prophecy,
the peaceloving fire
displaced in his rafters.

The banging of shields,
plastic and leather,
rang in his ears:

war war war sle sle sle
went the childish wailing of sirens
in the gusting wood,
and the night's drunken instruments

scoured the wet streets
for the Welsh doggis and their whelps.

An English city listens behind curtains
to the running and breathing, the slugging
thud of quarry cornered and floored:
the resistance is
that we will not turn the television up
in tribute to the night.

Divided loyalties, undermined
meal-tickets, sprouted on hillsides,
the weeds Indignation
twined with deep-rooted Ambivalence

picked for the same dish.
Drenched resisters sidled in droves
along valleys to give themselves up
to the straggling columns of troops and grain.

When the fighting is over, the land of dreams
is a table lit with unshareable faces,
a once-in-a-lifetime
remembered meal to the hungry:

a looted peacock under the arm
of some big, sharp-featured
father of mine
who dried his eyes at the flame of Sycharth.

Then the withdrawal to memory
of the fair people, walled in the clouds
of exile within, the retreat to mystery
of the fair times on their vague upland tracks.

Glyndŵr had to master this potent
trick of retirement, to the light
in a dolmen glimpsed rarely and late,
a light in the mind

where sometimes he lingers noisily in the grid of years
and the speed and charisma growl in him
to the applause of the shingle in the undertow,
old chimera whose wait has a tide's hypnotic

push still. It breaks
in like the sudden clatter of leaves
of a kneeling army

or a belief in the mountains upturned,
with mirrors,
lit from inside with our own light.

Steve Griffiths

The poem uses the chant of the northern English students at Oxford, heard
by Adam of Usk, at the beginning of the Glyndŵr uprising:

> *War war war, sle sle sle*
> *the Welsh doggis and their whelps.*

Bequeathed

Rearing horses claw the night air
like branches in a ruffled rasping tree;
red nostrilled and eyes white as snowdrops
reflect the fire of torches as poor people
    flee and the occupiers brave death, tribute
for their monarch, amid the exalted shouts of
Glyndŵr

who masked and deadly as a poisonous snake slash the
    occupier: the alien in his claimed land is halted
for a time by a people for once united by a renegade
King's man, his warfare training imploding on his
    tutors.

Honoured by posterity
a conquered land's last disciple
like a raging wind then, now a gentle breeze
dancing on the pages of history
reminding us of faltering sons and daughters
who court a foreign apron
like a Judas they cannot flourish
because of the vice-like grip of Glyndŵr's
belief in free spirits, people and lands.

Robert King

Í Owaín Glyndŵr

Byd dudrist, bywyḍ hydraul
Ydyw hwn hyd y daw haul.
Llawn yw, ac nid llawen neb,
A llonaid y naill wyneb
O dda i rai nid oedd raid;
Aml iawn gan y mileiniaid
Ariant ac aur, ni roent ged,
A golud, byd gogaled;
Cymru rhag maint eu camrwysg,
Cenedl druain fel brain brwysg,
Gallwn, nid erfyniwn fudd,
Eu galw yn gallor goludd.
A fu isaf ei foesau
Uchaf yw, mawr yw'r och fau:
A'r uchaf cyn awr echwydd
Isaf ac ufuddaf fydd.
A fu dincwd, hwd hudawl,
Y sy bencwd, tancwd diawl;
Myned yn weilch bob eilchwyl
Mae'r beryon culion cwyl;
Hyn a wna, hen a newydd,
Y drygfyd. Pa ryw fyd fydd?
Methu y mae y ddaear
Hyd nad oes nac ŷd nac âr.
Cadarnaf blaenaf un blaid

O fryd dyn fu Frytaniaid,
Adgnithion wedi cnithiaw
Ynt weithian, cywoedran Caw.
Tri amherodr tra moroedd
A fu onaddun', un oedd
Brenin brwydr, Brân briodawr,
Brawd Beli camwri mawr.
Cystennin a wnaeth drin draw,
Arthur, chwith fu neb wrthaw.
Diau o beth ydyw bod
Brenhinoedd, i'n bro hynod,
Bum hugain ar Lundain lys,
Coronog, ceirw yr ynys.
Oes farchawg urddawl, hawl hy,
Trais ac amraint, tros Gymru,
Ond Dafydd, uswydd aesawr,
Ustus a meddiannus mawr,
O Hanmer, llwydner llednais,
A Grigor, ail Sain Siôr Sais,
Er pan estynnwyd rhwyd trin
Gwayw ufelfellt gafaelfin,
A phensel Syr Hywel hoyw
Air Otiel , aur ei otoyw?
Bu amser caid blinder blwng
Anystwyth cyn ei ostwng.
Lle profed gerllaw Profyns,
Llew praff yn gwarchadw llu pryns;
Diwedd farchog, deddf orchest,
Dewredd grym, dur oedd ei grest,

O hil Ednowain hoywlyw
Hyd yr aeth ei had a'i ryw
Nid bu genedl ddiledlyth
Heb adu neb yn y nyth
A gwarthol loyw, os hoyw swydd,
Oreuraid ar ei orwydd.
Pa un weithion, pan ethyw,
Piau'r swydd? parhäus yw:
Owain, mael ni wn i mwy,
Iôr Glyn daeardor Dyfrdwy;
Arglwyddfab o ryw gwleddfawr
Sycharth cadfuarth ced fawr.
Henyw, hen ei ryw erioed
Er cyn cof a'r can cyfoed,
O Gymro, fam dinam dad;
Gwisgo wrls ac ysgarlad,
A harnais aur goreuryw,
A gra mân, barwn grym yw.
Os iach a rhydd fydd efô,
Ef a ennill, pan fynno,
Esgidiau, gwindasau gwaisg,
Cordwalfrith, carw diwylfraisg,
Yn ymwan ar dwrneimant
Yn briwio cyrff, yn bwrw cant;
Eistedd a gaiff ar osteg
Ar y bwrdd tâl, byrddaid teg;
Anneddf a cham ni oddef,
Ymysg ieirll ydd ymwaisg ef.

Gruffudd Llwyd

I Owain Glyndŵr

Eryr digrif afrifed,
Owain helm gain hael am ged,
Eurfab, agwrdd ei arfod,
Gruffudd Fychan, glân ei glod;
Mur Glyn, menestr rhoddlyn rhydd,
Dyfrdwy fawr dwfr diferydd:
Llafar ymannos noswaith
Oeddwn wrth gyfedd medd maith,
Fy nghrair, i'th aml gellweiriaw
I'th lys, lle cawn win o'th law;
Medd fynfyr, mwy oedd f'anfoes
A gwaeth dros fy maeth fy moes,
Nêr mawlair nawrym milwr,
Nag ar fy nhad, arnad, ŵr.
Yr awr yr aethost ar ŵyth
Dir Prydyn, darpar adwyth,
Agos i hiraeth, gaeth gad,
A'm dwyn i farw amdanad.
Nid aeth dy gof drosof draw,
Aur baladr, awr heb wylaw;
Dagrau dros y grudd dugrych
Dyfriw glaw fal dwfr a'i gwlych.
Pan oedd drymaf fy nhrafael
Amdanad, mab y tad hael,
Cefais o ben rhyw gennad,
Cei ras Duw cywir ystad,

Cael yn yr aer, calon rwydd,
Ohonod fawrglod, f'arglwydd.
Daroganawdd drymlawdd dro
Duw a dyn o doud yno,
F'enaid uwch Dyfrdwy faenawr,
Fy nêr, fwrw llawer i'r llawr.
Dewin, os mi a'i dywawd,
Fûm yma gwarwyfa gwawd.
Cefaist ramant yn d'antur
Uthr Bendragon, gofion gur,
Pan ddialawdd, gawdd goddef,
Ei frawd â'i rwysg ei frwydr ef.
Hwyliaist siwrneiaist helynt
Owain ab Urien gain gynt,
Pan oedd fuan ymwanwr
Y marchog duog o'r dŵr;
Gŵr fu ef wrth ymguraw
A phen draig y ffynon draw;
Gwŷr a fuant, llwyddiant llu,
Gwrdd ddewrnerth gwewyr ddyrnu.
Tithau Owain, taith ewybr,
Taer y gwnaut drafn â llafn llwybr.
Brawd unweithred y'th edir,
Barwn hoff, mab Urien hir,
Pan gyrhaeddawdd, ryglawdd rôn,
A phen marchog y ffynnon.
Pan oedd drymaf dy lafur
Draw yn ymwriaw â'r mur,
Torres dy onnen gennyd,

Tirion grair taer yn y gryd,
Dewredd Ffwg, dur oedd ei phen,
Dors garw yn dair ysgyren.
Gwelodd pawb draw i'th law lân,
Gwiw fawldaith, gwayw ufeldan;
Drylliaist, duliaist ar dalwrn,
Dy ddart hyd ymron dy ddwrn.
O nerth ac arial calon,
A braich ac ysgwydd a bron,
Peraist fy naf o'th lafur
Pyst mellt rhwng y dellt a'r dur;
Gyrraist yno, gwrs doniog,
Y llu, gyriad ychen llog,
Bob ddau, bob tri, rhi rhoddfawr
Ar darf oll o'r dyrfa fawr.
Hyd dydd brawd, medd dy wawdydd,
Hanwyd o feilch, hynod fydd,
Dyfyn glwys, dau finiog lain,
Dêl brwydr dy hwyl i Brydain,
Wrth dorri brisg i'th wisg wen
A'th ruthr i'r maes a'th rethren,
A'th hyrddwayw rhudd, cythrudd cant,
A'th ddeg enw a'th ddigoniant;
Clywsam, ddinam ddaioni,
Hort teg gan herod i ti,
Iach wyd, ddiarswyd ddursiamp,
A chrio i Gymro'r gamp:
A gawr drist gwedi'r garw dro
Brydnawn am Brydyn yno,

A'r gair i Gymru, hy hwyl,
Wyth archoll brwydr, o'th orchwyl,
A'r gwiw rwysg, a'r goresgyn,
A'r glod i'r marchog o'r Glyn.

Gruffudd Llwyd

Remembrance

And if we brought you home my Lord
Where would you rest.
A city? Yes we have a few.
But they once held your enemies
And enmity still lingers there.

To Gwynedd then, it still endures my Lord
Though battered through these years.
A huge slate statue could be raised
Where tourists could gaze and wonder
While they wandered through.

To Powys, where your Sycharth stood my Lord
Though nothing now remains,
No plaque or monument lies there.
Such a lonely place where only we
Who know, stand and remember.

To the south, the windswept valleys Lord
Where once your captains Kemys and Cadwgan
Swept down upon our armoured foes.
Destroyed them as they fled from you
In sight of Cardiff Castle walls.

Or should we leave you lie my Lord,
If where they say you lie is true.
It's in our souls remembrance lives,
We need no statue, stone, or grave
To visit, stare and bow our heads,
We need no monument of slate
Or marble monolith in City Halls
You'll live forever in our thoughts
As all our heroes gone before
So let your bones lie where they are
If where they say they lie is true
Your memory will be kept alive
Within our grateful hearts for ever more.

John Parry

OWAIN GLYNDŴR

Iolo Goch a Gruffydd Llwyd, beirdd y Gogledd,
  A olrheiniodd achau ei dad, a disgrifio ei Sycharth ef,
A dyma fardd o Forgannwg yn moli ei fam ef, Helen,
  Pendefiges yn llinach tywysogion a phendefigion y De.

Ni wyddys dim am ei hanes, ac ni ellir olrhain ei hachau,
  Ond gallwn ddychmygu mai hyhi a ddysgodd i'w mab
Hanes yr hen Brydain; yr ymdrech rhwng y ddwyddraig;
  Proffwydoliaeth y beirdd am arwr i adfer y wlad,
Y mab darogan, Arthur, neu Gynan neu Gadwaladr,
  Sôn am gyfreithiau Hywel Dda a oedd wedi aros
Yn eu grym yn hwy nag yn y Gogledd.

Methu yn y diwedd ar ôl buddugoliaethau'r Cymry
A wnaeth y gwrthryfel, er gwaethaf help y sêr,
Y tywydd, y Ffrancod, y Llydawiaid a'r bradwyr,
A gorfoleddu a wnaeth y Saeson yn eu buddugoliaeth aflêr
A''r Saeson yn rhoi ffrwyn yn llawer tynnach ar eu gwar
Gan wahardd pob segurwr, tramp, cyfarwydd a bardd.

Abad Glyn Rhosyn a ddwedodd wrtho ar y Berwyn
  Ei fod wedi codi ganrif yn rhy gynnar cyn torri o'r wawr,
Ond, o ludw ei frwydrau y cododd ym mhen canrif
  Fel y ffenics, ei ysbryd i'n harwain ni'n awr.

Cilio ar ddifancoll â'i ddraig aur a wnaeth y dewin,
A'i Sycharth yn adfeilion, a'i genedl yn drist ei gwedd,
A thrueni na wyddom lle y mae ef, a Gruffudd a Helen
Yn gorwedd, i ni gael plannu'r ddraig goch ar eu bedd.

Hyhi a roes y De a Dinefwr iddo yn filwyr,
A'i dysg yn y Brut a roddes iddo ei ddraig;
Ac ar gynllun y Gynhadledd yn Nhŷ Gwyn ar Daf
Y cododd yn Harlech a Machynlleth ei seneddau Cymreig.

Gwenallt

Owain Glyndŵr

I ddifancoll y ciliodd Owain,
  Yn ôl tystiolaeth y brut,
A thrueni nad ychwanegodd hefyd
  Ym mha le a pha sut:
Ai yn Monnington Straddel gydag Alis
  Y cafodd ar y diwedd do?
Ai wrth y capel gerllaw y gorwedd
  Yn heddwch Seisnig y gro?
    Ond fe gododd ymhen pedair canrif
    I gychwyn ei frwydr drachefn.

Ei blasty di-glo, diglicied
  A losgwyd yn lludw gwyn;
Parlyswyd y clomennod yn y maendwr
  A chrynodd y pysod yn y llyn:
Cymerwyd yr orau o'r gwragedd
  I Lundain, a dau o'i blant,
Ac yntau fel Grivas yn cael ei hela
  Gan y gormeswyr o fryn i bant:
    Ond fe gododd ymhen pedair canrif
    I gychwyn ei frwydr drachefn.

Mynnai gael Eglwys y Cymry
  Yn rhydd o afael Caer-gaint;
Codi dau Goleg i'r ysgolheigion

A chael Esgobion Cymraeg i'r saint:
A theyrnasodd am dro fel brenin,
  Yn null y tywysogion gynt;
Ond y pedwar llew a orchfygwyd
  A'r sêr, y glaw a'r gwynt:
      Ond fe gododd ymhen pedair canrif
      I gychwyn ei frwydr drachefn.

Sefydliad erbyn hyn yw ei Senedd
  I gynnal cyfarfodydd y dref,
A rhoddwyd bordydd, chwarae biliards
  A chaffe hefyd ynddo ef:
A chlywyd yn ddiweddar am y ffrwgwd
  Rhwng y Cymry eang a chul,
A ddylid agor y caffe
  Ar brynhawn dydd Sul?
      Ond fe gyfyd ymhen y canrifoedd
      I agor ei Senedd drachefn.

Gwenallt

On the Dedication of the Sword of State of Cymru

The Royal Standard of England bears:
St George's Flag of England,
St Andrew's Flag of Scotland,
And St Patrick's Flag of Ireland.

St David's Flag of Wales
Has never been included.
Our Welsh Flag,
The Flag of Cadwaladr,
Y Ddraig Goch
Is the oldest national flag in the world.

A Nation has its own flag.

The Royal Coat of Arms bears:
The three lions of England,
The lion of Scotland,
And the harp of Ireland.

Glyndŵr's Coat of Arms
Is the four lions rampant
Of the House of Gwynedd –
The oldest royal house in Britain.

A Nation has its own Coat of Arms.

The Royal Coat of Arms
Bears the symbols of:
The rose of England
The thistle of Scotland,
And the shamrock of Ireland.

The British have their older symbols:
St Peter's leek, the daffodil of spring,
St David's leek of victory over the Saxon,
And the dragon of Cadwaladr.

A Nation has its own symbols.

The Great Sword of State
Carries the motifs of:
The portcullis of Westminster,
The rose of England,
The fleur de lys of France,
The thistle of Scotland
And the harp of Ireland.

There is no symbol
Of Power
Or Authority
Over Wales,
The British precursor of England.
The First Nation wants
The symbol of authority
Of its Great Sword of State.

A Nation needs its own sword.

The trinity of sword, flag and coat of arms
Is now complete.

A Nation, not a principality.
Cymru not Wales.
Comrades not foreigners.
Cymraeg not Welsh.

The British people,
The First Nation,
Is moving…
Again.

Terry Breverton

The Poets and the Poems

NIGEL JENKINS is a lecturer and writer. He has written site-specific poetry for locations in Swansea and elsewhere, and frequently gives public readings of his work. His poem 'Llywelyn ap Gruffydd Fychan' is an emotional piece about a man of great courage who sacrificed himself. This poem was commissioned for the unveiling of a memorial to Llywelyn at Llanymddyfri on October 6, 2001.

MIKE JENKINS is a poet and story writer. His poem 'Glyndŵr Road' is a contemporary piece examining the legacy of Glyndŵr and looking to the future.

HARRI WEBB lived from 1920 to 1994 and published more than 350 poems. Swansea born, and educated at Oxford, he was a poet, journalist, public speaker, Welsh Republican, essayist and scriptwriter. Fiercely political, he was the 'people's poet'.

R. S. THOMAS was born in Cardiff and educated at University College of North Wales, Bangor. He died at the age of 87 on 25 September, 2000. Wales' greatest 20th century poet, his three very different classics about Owain Glyndŵr appear in this anthology.

A. G. PRYS-JONES was born in Denbigh, North Wales in 1888 and died in 1987 in Kingston upon Thames. He was educated at Pontypridd Grammar School, Llandovery College and Jesus College, Oxford. A poet, broadcaster, critic, dramatist, educationist and historian, his three extremely moving, classic songs for Owain enrich this tribute.

TERRY BREVERTON is the founder of Wales Books (Glyndŵr Publishing). 'Nationalism' was taken from his collection *The Path to Inexperience*. 'Rebirth' was written for this anthology, while 'On the Dedication of the Sword of State of Cymru' was written for the unveiling of the sword at Cardiff Castle on 6 May 2004.

BYRON BEYNON lives in Swansea. His work has appeared in several publications, ranging from the *Independent* to *Planet*, *Stand Magazine* to *Poetry Ireland*, *The Red Wheelbarrow* to *Quadrant* (Australia). He is currently a member of the editorial board of Roundy House magazine, and tutors for the University of Wales, Swansea.

KEN JONES on 'A Dried Deer Skin': 'This poem is a haibun celebrating Owain's first victory, at Hyddgen. A haibun is an ancient Japanese literary genre which blends haiku with haiku-like prose. Basho's *Narrow Road to the Deep North*, composed in the 17th century, is perhaps the best known example. The genre is now being revived and extensively developed by the western haiku community, and the time is ripe to introduce it to the wider public. And as regards Owain Glyndŵr, Iron Press have just published a collection of my Welsh interest haibun and haiku entitled *Stallion's Crag*. The centrepiece is a 6,000 word haibun celebrating the landscape, history and legends of Plynlimon (Pumlumon Fawr). Needless to say, Owain features strongly in this, as also my hermit cave on Craig y March, associated with the hero's charger. Owain almost certainly slept in my cave (the best on the mountain!) – as did doubtless also Saint Curig, Lewys Glyncothi and many other poets, patriots and outlaws. This collection also includes a short haibun celebrating another Glyndŵr victory, at Pilleth.' (*Stallion's Crag* is obtainable for £6.50 post-free from Iron Press, 5 Marden Terrace, Cullercoats, NE30 4PD.)

ALAN WYKE wrote his poem 'Sycharth' one evening as the dusk embraced the home of the last 'real' Prince of Wales.

Iolo Goch oedd bardd mawl mwyaf y 14eg ganrif. Ef oedd bardd Owain, ac mae tair o'i glasuron yn y casgliad. Roedd Iolo wedi achub bywyd Owain cyn i'r gwrthryfel ddechrau, pan oedd gelyn Glyndŵr, Lord Grey, wedi cuddio dynion yn y goedwig o gwmpas cartref Glyndŵr. Roedd Lord Grey yn gallu siarad Cymraeg, felly adroddodd Iolo ddarn o gynghanedd o flaen y ddau, gan gynnwys neges gudd yn y gerdd i Owain am y perygl. Esgusododd Owain ei hun, a dianc trwy'r cefn.

Mae **Menna Elfyn** yn fardd, dramodydd ac awdur llawn amser. Cyhoeddodd nifer o gyfrolau o farddoniaeth, ac mae'n teithio'r byd yn darllen ei barddoniaeth. Mae ei cherdd 'Catrin Glyndŵr' yn sôn am ferch Owain, a gipiwyd i Dŵr Llundain a'i charcharu yno.

Gillian Clarke is a poet, playwright, editor and translator (from Welsh). Her poem 'The Exile's Song' is a translation from the Welsh of Menna Elfyn.

Steve Griffiths was born in Trearddur Bay. He is a social researcher in London. He has published four collections of poetry, the latest, *Selected Poems* with Seren. He is a fellow of the Welsh Academy.

Robert King lives in the Vale of Neath. He is a lecturer in Welsh history, and has published six or seven volumes on local history. His poems have been published in various magazines.

Gruffudd Llwyd oedd hoff fardd Owain Glyndŵr, ac un o feirdd pwysicaf ei gyfnod. Mae ei ddau gywydd mawl i Owain o'r cyfnod cyn dechrau'r gwrthryfel wedi'u cynnwys yn y llyfr.

John Parry's 'Remembrance' is his first published poem.

Gwenallt yw'r bardd mwyaf yr iaith Gymraeg, yn ôl llawer. Fe'i ganwyd dros ganrif yn ôl, ac mae dau glasur o'i waith am Owain wedi'u cynnwys yn y llyfr.

Owain Glyndŵr Ten Pound Note

Designed by Siôn Jones;
Five notes in a presentation wallet
£4.50

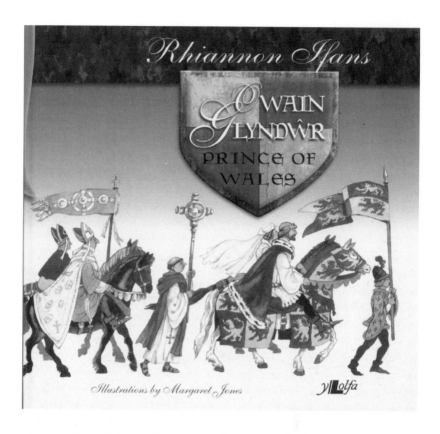

Illustrations by Margaret Jones

Owain Glyndŵr: Prince of Wales

Rhiannon Ifans

0 86243 535 8

£5.95

Owain Glyn Dŵr:
Trwy Ras Duw, Tywysog Cymru
R. R. Davies
0 86243 625 7
£6.95

Owain Glyndŵr Stamps

To commemorate the 600th anniversary
of his revolution

£2.00 for a sheet of 20

Patriotic Poster

by Paul Nicholls, with a quotation from the work of Gerallt
Lloyd Owen

£3.95

A Dragon to Agincourt

Action-packed historical novel
set during Glyndŵr's revolution

0 86243 684 2

£7.95

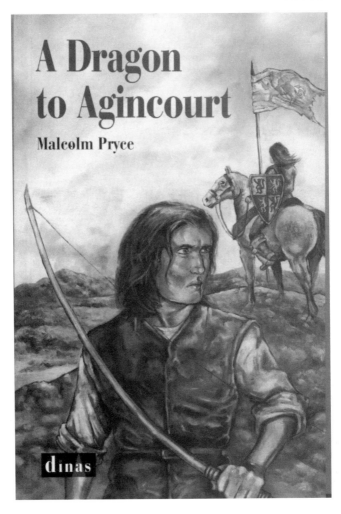

Titles already published

Shapeshifters at Cilgerran	Liz Whittaker £5.95
Germs	Dai Vaughan £5.95
Until Aber Falls Into the Sea	Frances Myers £9.95
Cunval's Mission	David Hancocks £5.95
When the Kids Grow Up	Ken James £6.95
The Church Warden	Lillian Comer £7.95
The Fizzing Stone	Liz Whittaker £4.95
A Dragon To Agincourt	Malcom Pryce £7.95
Aberdyfi: Past and Present	Hugh M Lewis £6.95
Aberdyfi: The Past Recalled	Hugh M Lewis £6.95
Ar Bwys y Ffald	Gwilym Jenkins £7.95
Blodeuwedd	Ogmore Batt £5.95
Black Mountains	David Barnes £6.95
Choose Life!	Phyllis Oostermeijer £5.95
Clare's Dream	J Gillman Gwynne £4.95
Cwpan y Byd a dramâu eraill	J O Evans £4.95
Dragonrise	David Morgan Williams £4.95
Dysgl Bren a Dysgl Arian	R Elwyn Hughes £9.95
In Garni's Wake	John Rees £7.95
Stand Up and Sing	Beatrice Smith £4.95
The Dragon Wakes	Jim Wingate £6.95
The Wonders of Dan yr Ogof	Sarah Symons £6.95
You Don't Speak Welsh	Sandi Thomas £5.95
Barking Mad	Philip Lemon £5.95

*For more information
about this innovative imprint,
contact Lefi Gruffudd at
lefi@ylolfa.com
or go to www.ylolfa.com/dinas.
A Dinas catalogue
is also available.*